CITY I ❤ LOVE

POEMS BY LEE BENNETT HOPKINS

ILLUSTRATED BY MARCELLUS HALL

Abrams Books for Young Readers, New York

The illustrations in this book were made with
brush and ink and watercolor on paper.

Library of Congress Cataloging-in-Publication Data

Hopkins, Lee Bennett.
City I love / by Lee Bennett Hopkins ; illustrated by Marcellus Hall.
p. cm.
ISBN 978-0-8109-8327-4
1. Cities and towns—Juvenile poetry. 2. City and town life—Juvenile poetry.
3. Children's poetry, American. I. Hall, Marcellus, ill. II. Title.

PS3558.O63544C58 2009
811'.54—dc22
2008008226

Book design by Chad W. Beckerman

Printed and bound in China
10 9 8 7 6 5 4 3 2 1

Abrams Books for Young Readers are available at special discounts when purchased
in quantity for premiums and promotions as well as fundraising or educational
use. Special editions can also be created to specification. For details, contact
specialmarkets@hnabooks.com or the address below.

MAY - - 2009

HNA ▪▪▪▪
harry n. abrams, inc.
a subsidiary of La Martinière Groupe
115 West 18th Street
New York, NY 10011
www.hnabooks.com

To Tamar Brazis, Howard Reeves, and
Jason Wells—who epitomize *city*
—L.B.H.

To Jessica, Natalie, Diego, and Lola
—M.H.

SING A SONG OF CITIES

Sing a song of cities.
If you do,
Cities will sing back
                    to you.

They'll sing in subway roars and rumbles,
People-laughs, machine-loud grumbles.

Sing a song of cities.
If you do,
Cities will sing back.

Cities will sing back
                    to you.

CITY

Mile-long skyscrapers are my trees.
Subway's *whoosh*—my summer breeze.

A hydrant is my swimming pool
Where friends and I find some cool.

City is the place to be.
City is the place for me.

HYDRANT

I wonder
whether

pouring
roaring
gushing
rushing
water

spouting
from our
corner hydrant

flows
from here—

goes
so far—

to cause
lazy Venetian gondolas
to bob and float

as easily as our
homemade
wooden-popsicle-boat.

FROM THE GROUND

Look!

    Up there!

High up there
where
men and women
building the new skyscraper

    balance on beams
    dangle on derricks
    glide on girders
    sway on concrete slabs.

Amazing!
    Breathtaking!
        Wondrous!

Why,
it's like watching
a razzle-dazzle
razzmatazz
three-ring
steel circus
performance
appearing
in
the
sky.

MOTHER'S PLEA

Silence sirens.

Hush all horns.

Quiet rumbling

      traffic roars.

Please
city

      have
      some
      pity.

Promise me

      not
      one
      more
      beep?

My newborn

      pigeons
      need
      their
      sleep.

TAXI!

You stand
on a corner
shouting:

"Taxi!"

"Taxi!"

knowing
deep
inside
taxi cabs
never
stop
on
rainy
days.

SUBWAYS ARE PEOPLE

Subways are people—

    People standing
    People sitting
        People swaying to and fro
          Some in suits
          Some in tatters
            People I will never know.

          Subways are people—

           Some with glasses
           Some without
             Boy with smile
             Girl with frown

People dashing
Steel flashing
Up and down and round the town.

Subways are people—

People old
People new
People always on the go
Racing, running, rushing people
People I will never know.

CITY SUMMER

It is so hot.

So hot.

So very hot
even
the fiery
orange-red
sun
wears
a
sweatband
on
this
sultry
heat-filled
summer
day.

KITE

New kite
blue-white

  flitters
  twirls
  tumbles
  twitters

like
a
young bird

in
new morning's
wide-awake
city
sky.

GET 'EM HERE

"Hot dogs with sauerkraut
Cold drinks here!"

"Hot dogs with sauerkraut
Get 'em here!"

Shouts the man
as he rolls
city's smallest store
all tucked neatly
under
a huge, blue-orange striped
umbrella.

SPARROW

Lucky to be born
on this balcony, sparrow
awaits city flights.

MERRY-GO-ROUND HORSE

Merry-go-round horse
has
tears
in
its
eyes
left
by
spring
rain.

SEAL AT THE ZOO

I like to

    watch
    look at
    see

that big
old lazy
black-as-silk
seal

hoping
maybe
just
one day

I can

    touch
    and pet
    and feel.

BRIDGE

Even
the strongest
men
in the world

cannot
hold
as much
steel
as you
can
at
one
time.

CITY LIGHTS

Blazing lights

    flicker
    flash
    glitter
    gleam
    twinkle
    sparkle
    bedazzle
    beam

    so

    brilliantly
    bright.

Reasons
why
city
stays
awake
all
night.

WINTER

NEVER

EVER

quarrel

with

winter.

It

ALWAYS

wins.

SNOW CITY

Snow glides quietly

d
  o
    w
      n

Filling air
    with a magical

    hush—

But tomorrow the snow
    will make everyone frown

For streets will be filled
    with a magical

    M U S H.

CITY I LOVE

In the city
I live in—
city I love—
mornings wake
to swishes, swashes,
sputters
of sweepers
swooshing litter
from gutters.

In the city
I live in—
city I love—
afternoons pulse
with
people hurrying,
scurrying—
races of faces
pacing to
must-get-there
places.

In the city
I live in—
city I love—
nights shimmer
with lights
competing
with stars
above
unknown heights.

In the city
I live in—
city I love—
as dreams
start to creep
my city
of senses
lulls
me
to
sleep.